1/02

Fossil Ridge Public Library District
Braidwood, IL 60408

Learning How to Stay Safe at School

Susan Kent

The Rosen Publishing Group's
PowerKids Press™
New York

For Bob Larson and Barbara Rubin, good friends in safety and in danger.

Published in 2001 by The Rosen Publishing Group, Inc.
29 East 21st Street, New York, NY 10010

First Edition

Book Design: Maria E. Melendez

Photo Credits: Cover and title page pp.1, 4, 7, 8, 11, 12, 15, 16, 19 by Bonnie Rothstein-Brewer; pp. 20 © Skjold Photography.

Kent, Susan, 1942–
    Learning how to stay safe at school / Susan Kent.
        p. cm.— (The violence prevention library)
    Includes index.
    Summary: Describes a variety of ways to cope with problems that children face at school, including peer pressure, bullying behavior, and drug dealing.
    ISBN 0-8239-5616-4
    1. School Violence—Prevention—Juvenile literature [1. School violence] I. Title II. Series
LB3013.3.K45 2000
371.7'82—dc21   00-023839

Manufactured in the United States of America

Contents

Maria

Maria does not feel safe at school. A few girls pick on her. They call her names and bump into her in the hallways. They even pull her hair in class. Maria tells her teacher. Her teacher moves the girls to different desks. This helps inside the classroom, but not outside. When Maria joins the school **orchestra**, she makes new friends. She walks with them in the hallways and sits with them at lunch. Her new friends stand up for her when the mean girls bother her. Soon the girls stop picking on her. Maria now likes going to school.

This girl is sad because she is being picked on in the schoolyard.

Rules at School

It is important to feel safe at school. Your teacher and principal help **protect** you. They make rules to keep you safe. Walking slowly in the hallways is a rule that can prevent accidents. Fire drills also help keep you safe. During a fire drill, you have to follow the rules. This means listening to your teacher and staying with your class. Fire drills let you practice leaving the building quickly and calmly. You should always listen to your teacher and follow the rules at school.

It is important to listen carefully to instructions during a fire drill. ▶

Getting to School Safely

It is important to stay safe on the way to school. If you walk to school, always follow the **route** your parents picked out for you. It is a good idea to walk with a friend. If you have to go alone, get to school on time so you do not have to wait outside by yourself. It is important that you never talk to or take a ride from a stranger. If you take the bus, wait until the bus has come to a complete stop before you get on or off. On the bus, be sure to stay in your seat and face forward. Never stick your hands out the window, and always listen to the bus driver.

These two boys feel safe knowing they can walk to and from school together.

When Someone Picks on You

It can be hard to get kids to stop picking on you at school. You may have to try out many ideas before you find one that works. Ignoring the kids who pick on you or asking them to stop might help. If you say, "Stop it!" in a loud voice, other classmates might notice and stand up for you. Perhaps the troublemakers will feel **embarrassed** and leave. Staying with a group of friends rather than alone often helps. Humor sometimes helps. If you tell jokes when someone picks on you, that person might think he or she is not bothering you and might leave you alone.

Staying with friends might stop ▶
others from picking on you.

Avoiding Trouble

Another way to stay safe at school is to avoid trouble. You will probably get to know which kids are usually looking for a fight. Be sure to stay away from them. If you are not near them, they cannot bother you.

Sometimes you can stop trouble before it starts. When classmates want to pick a fight with you or your friends, try to talk about the problem calmly. If they say something mean, do not say something mean back. Instead ask, "Why did you say that? Can we talk about this?" If they will not talk, try to leave the area with your friends as soon as you can.

◀ *If you see people fighting, you should walk away and tell an adult.*

Peer Pressure

Since you want your friends to like you, you may think you have to do whatever they do. This is called **peer pressure**, and it can get you into a lot of trouble. Sometimes friends want to do something you think is not safe. They might even dare you to do it, but don't! Remember, always do what you think is right, no matter what your friends say. Do not let them talk you into doing something you think is not safe. What other people think of you is not as important as staying safe. When you do what is right, you can feel good about yourself.

When you do what you think is right, you feel good about yourself and you stay safe. ▸

Doing the Right Thing

There are many things you can do to stay safe at school. Some are easy, like staying healthy and busy. Join clubs and after-school activities. Be on a sports team or in a drama group. Make friends with people who do what you like to do. Some things are harder to do. If you have groups or gangs in your school that are violent and pick on kids, you and your friends might want to start a "Be Safe" club. You can make posters and pass out flyers asking kids to **respect** each other. If you help make your school a safer place, you will feel **proud** of yourself.

◄ *Joining clubs and making friends is a good way to stay safe at school.*

Asking for Help

Although there are many things you can do to stay safe at school, sometimes you need to ask for help. Some problems are too big for you and your friends to solve. It is important to find an adult you **trust** to ask for help. You should tell a teacher if you see a fight between classmates. Tell your teacher, **guidance counselor**, or principal if you see anyone with drugs. You should also tell an adult if you know someone has brought a weapon to your school. It is okay to ask for help when you see a problem you cannot solve on your own.

If you have problems at school, it is important to ask for help. ▶

Danny

Danny sees two teenagers hanging around the schoolyard. One of them has a knife. A few kids talk to them for a while and then hurry away. Danny learns from friends that the teens are selling drugs. His friends say anyone who tells will get hurt. Danny does not feel good about this. He knows drugs are bad for you and against the law. He also worries about the knife. Danny thinks about who can help. He finally decides to tell his guidance counselor. Soon Danny notices that the drug dealers do not come to the schoolyard anymore.

Danny feels safer at school now that he knows his guidance counselor got rid of the drug dealers in the schoolyard.

21

Emergencies

No matter how well anyone plans, a **disaster** can still strike. For instance, a tornado, earthquake, hurricane, or flood could strike your school. The kind of **emergency** that could happen may depend on where you live. A fire, though, can happen anywhere. If you see a fire, no matter how small, be sure to report it right away. In any disaster, always stay calm. Listen to the adults and follow their instructions. Whether it is an emergency or an ordinary day, following rules and paying attention can help you stay safe at school.

Glossary

disaster (dih-ZAS-ter) An event that causes suffering or loss.

embarrassed (im-BAYR-ist) Feeling ashamed.

emergency (ih-MUR-jin-see) An event that happens with little or no warning, where help is needed very fast.

guidance counselor (GY-dins KOWN-suh-ler) Someone who helps students solve problems.

orchestra (OR-kehs-truh) A group of musicians that play music together.

peer pressure (PEER PREH-sher) The strong influence friends or classmates can have over you.

protect (pruh-TEKT) To keep from harm or danger.

proud (PROWHD) Pleased and confident about doing something well.

respect (ree-SPEKT) To think highly of someone.

route (ROOT) The path you take to get somewhere.

trust (TRUHST) Knowing that you can count on someone to be honest and not hurt you.

Index